Wes

Walker

A Blueprint for Government that Doesn't Suck

Volume 2 of the Doug Giles Contra Mundum Collection

Published by White Feather Press.
(www.whitefeatherpress.com)

ISBN 978-1-61808-095-0

Printed in the United States of America

Cover design by David Bugnon and mobopolis.com

White Feather Press

Reaffirming Faith in God, Family, and Country!

Dedication

It is impossible to list or even imagine the different influences and factors that need to line up in a person's life before a project like this can come together. But among them all, a few certainly do stand out, and I would be remiss not to acknowledge them.

Much of this book is centered on "questions" and "convictions". Much of what I know about both of these I owe to my parents. Thank you.

I might never have persevered through the many rewrites and edits had I not been given a love for writing. A gift for which I am indebted to many of my teachers, but in particular, Mrs. Laverne Noble and Mrs. Jane Ripkens. Thank you.

My thoughts and ideas would have been lost in some obscure corner of cyberspace had I not partnered with the Clashdaily team and White Feather Press. Thank you.

Above all, I am grateful for the wonderful support of the best wife a man could wish for.

It is to you, Karen,
that I dedicate this book.

Contents

Introduction

It is sometimes easier, when people are entrenched in their politics, to find common ground on what they hate rather than on what they like. If pollsters actually asked plain-language questions that mattered, for example, "What sucks?" could people agree on an answer?

The most popular answer just might be "the way things are now" (i.e., status quo). I'm not even kidding. Could you find any level of government – anywhere – where people would say "these guys have got everything sorted out, I can't think of any way to make it better."

Of course the unity falls apart when you ask how they should fix it, but we can all pretty much agree that "something" needs fixing.

How can we build on that? How about the idea that given a choice between making life better or worse for its citizens, the government should always choose "better". Sure, not everyone will define "better" or "worse" the same way, but we're talking big picture here.

So, the status quo sucks, and needs fixing. Got it. So, now what?

The experts suck too. Or at least some

of them do, otherwise everybody would agree about what sucks and how to fix it. The fact that they fight about what sucks and how to fix it means that at least some of them (maybe all?) are part of the problem. Because they suck too.

So, if our experts (politicians, pundits, lobbyists and laymen, the whole bunch) suck at least half of the time, we're gonna need a way to figure out what doesn't suck.

We'll have to do it the old-school way, by thinking for ourselves. The experts are the experts for one reason. They tell Joe Average that they do a special kind of thinking the rest of us can't do for ourselves, and, like chumps, we let them. So if we just "trust them" we won't need to think or reason for ourselves. Well then, how well has "trusting them" worked out so far? Right, we already covered that.

What if I told you that most of these people aren't any smarter than Joe Citizen? Or if I said that any of us can think through the big issues we normally let them handle on our behalf? If you can cut big issues down to bite-sized ideas, and get a good look at them, you can judge for yourself what the problems are, and how to solve them.

But where would you begin? No two people have the same "how to fix this mess" lists and we could never look at them all anyway. If we tried it that way, we'd be doomed from the start. We need a shortcut to get right to the point. A shortcut like when we reduced fractions to the "lowest common denominator" back in math class.

Simplifying issues can be handled by grouping ideas into categories and working with general principles instead of specific cases. This will get us to the big picture sooner.

If we do this right, we'll get a rough sketch of the competing ideas, and can see which side has solutions we think don't suck. Or at least (since the world isn't perfect) solutions that only suck a little.

So, are we back to the tired old "Left" and "Right" standoff? No. Because Left and Right suck too.

When you come right down to it, really, what use are those labels? If there was some other way to identify yourself politically, who'd pick that? They're both political train wrecks. Most of the time, the devoted activists join the side opposite the things they hate, while others walk away from the whole process completely. It's like that old Churchill quote, "... democracy is the worst form of government except for all the others that have been tried."

Even if you wanted to cheer one team on, do the names even mean anything? Using the American example (but anywhere else could work, too) Blue Dog Democrats are practically Republicans and Republicans-in-Name-Only (RINOs) could join the DNC without changing their convictions. So what's the point?

During elections, cynics complain there is no difference between Left and Right. One is driving the country off a cliff at top speed – and the other, at about half as fast. If the car's been crashed, who cares whether Thelma or Louise was the one driving? We'll need a better way of sorting this out.

There's another very good reason to avoid using "Left" and "Right".

Familiar terms can close your mind. When the guy on your team is an idiot, you make excuses for him. When the other team's guy is an idiot, you want his head on a plate. You don't have to be a genius to realize that these biases won't lead to a fair assessment of facts. The same thing applies to ideas. When your guy's idea is lame, you make excuses. When the other guy's idea is fantastic, you look for problems with it. Our "tribal" political loyalties tend to blind us.

So how can we figure out what we're contrasting?

First, make it simple. Set up two teams and compare their strengths and weaknesses. The names of the groups are unimportant, since they're only being used loosely, more important is what they describe. They will need to be real, cohesive groups with something in common. (Here's another reason Right/Left just won't work.)

To make it fair, we need our starting point to be something they agree on (things that suck) so that when compare their solutions (things they say don't suck) we won't be comparing apples to oranges.

So what solidifies them into two distinct groups? One group likes government – they trust that it usually does the right thing, and is a positive force for good. The other group, not so much. For them it's like having a dingo for a guard dog – really good at keeping burglars out, but you're never quite sure when he's going to turn on you. They don't think government is bad, exactly. But it isn't necessarily good, either. Why? Government is made up of people. Any virtue or vice that can show up in a person, can also show up in a government. Because government is a big, faceless bureaucracy, where accountability is spotty, these defects can get magnified.

So then, one of our groups are fans of government involvement. Let's call them "Fans". It's a neutral name that describes them. They need their counterpart. An opposite of Fans can be tricky because it might slant your opinion. They're unconvinced that government is the solution. So understanding the word to mean that, let's go with "Doubters".

So far we've something we want to change – the status quo; and two groups with different ways to fix it.

We've managed to sidestep the left-right nonsense by picking names that mean something, that didn't exist before we started this, and don't bring baggage.

Now, before we can figure out how to make a government that doesn't suck, we will need to kick around some ideas about what qualities a government should have, and what tools can help us evaluate them.

CHAPTER 1 - SETUP

IF YOU WANTED TO BUILD SOME-thing – an engine, a computer pro-gram, a fitness routine, anything – wouldn't you sit down with a plan, to know what you wanted in a finished product before you start putting it together? Or would you start sticking random pieces together and hope you could modify it as you go?

You'd start with a plan, right? Have you noticed we never see that approach to politics? Instead we see people running in circles, reacting, throwing new laws on top of old ones without even making sure they fit together. Is this the best we can do? The success or failure of entire nations is hinged on what – a group of people who can't see past the next election? Does that seem like good planning?

Everyone seems to be working in dif-ferent directions with different agendas.

That's not such a good strategy. Do you remember why NASA lost a $125 Million Mars Orbiter? Teams were building with different units of measurement, and a "little mistake" wrecked the whole mission. But, guess what? Unlike government, at least the folks at NASA were all planning the same mission!

Where's this plan going to come from?

Before you build a big project, it's a good idea to make a small model of it. It lets you spot problems without wasting time and energy. Even Michelangelo made one for "David", and he was no rookie. But ideas aren't like buildings where we can create a mock-up either in a scale model, or digital. Ideas need a different model.

We've got a tool for that. It's one we've had throughout recorded history. Have you ever been immersed in a movie or a novel? You are seeing a world as it might exist, or maybe never could; a world where possibilities are limited only by the imaginations of the author and reader. Mix in some characters, and situations, and you have a functioning virtual reality. It's a laboratory where you can safely test-drive ideas, without having any failed experiments mess up your real world. We'll borrow that technique for our own ideas workshop.

Because there's so much room for "what-if" in science fiction, we'll borrow some ideas from there. But all good fiction can help us step into another world this way. It's what makes the classics so "classic".

A laboratory in our mind isn't new. Einstein used it to work out theories in his imagination long before anyone could prove them. Hollywood is forever building and destroying worlds. They tell us about life and the world as it might be, or even never could be, and let us take the ideas they're built on out for a test drive.

The movies *Star Trek*, *Firefly* and *Back to the Future* all tell stories about very different futures. None of them ever existed, but we can discuss them as if they were real. (If you don't believe me, look at the heat Obama took for using the phrase "Jedi Mind Meld" and accidentally blending *Star Trek* with *Star Wars*. They're only fiction, but to the diehard fans can seem so *very* real.)

Storylines for the future can run the whole gamut. Many of them are awesome filled with optimism and technological marvels, but some of them are dark and tragic, like zombie movies, end-of-world catastrophes, or *1984*. Each lets us look at life and problem-solving from a different angle.

It isn't useless escapism either, not usually. Often, our stories can give us new ideas on what's good, what isn't. They might tell us how we can make bad things better. Sometimes (like *Frankenstein*) it's about how good things can go bad.

Here's the good news. If the story goes south and the world blows up, nobody cares. It isn't your world. It isn't your fault. You don't have to fix it or blame someone else for what went wrong. If it goes wrong, just don't bring it into the real world. Just like a test drive ... you don't care if it's a lemon, because you don't own it.

Movies like *I Am Legend* or *Blade Runner* help you ask questions about what it means to be human. *Star Trek* or

Serenity can show different models of how we'll sort out Earth's future government. Or maybe it'll fall apart and be every man for himself like *The Road* or *Mad Max*.

Notice, I'm not just picking good movies. It doesn't have to be a good movie to be useful. *Judge Dredd* was brutal. It isn't about the acting or storyline, but the ideas. In this case, *Crime and Punishment* issues.

Life in *Judge Dredd's* future was horrible – but the audience was *supposed* to think that. Why? Life was safe and clean, but it was not free. Cars could drive you, but you couldn't drive them. There were so many limitations on individuality that it became intolerable. Let it prompt the question: how do we balance freedom with laws without either side going wrong? So stories, even this one, can be a tool for helping get our heads around big ideas.

What about *Star Trek*? Should we expect one-world government one day? Is it good, bad, or even realistic?

Will we fall to pieces like the zombie flicks or 80's dystopias? Will we see every-man-for-himself scenarios of roving tribes and gangs?

Did *Firefly* get it right blending America and China into a superculture? Or will life continue with the same old story of different powers rising and falling as time goes on?

For that, we'll have to head into the laboratory ourselves for some real-world imagining. To start us off, and give a platform to work from, I'll set up a scenario, and some starter questions. Like any lab work, you will be responsible for your own results. This is just to help get the ball rolling.

There's no rule saying this has to be dull, either. If the story is interesting, the experiment will be too. So instead of kicking around political theory, let's put together a scenario where we start with a blank canvas, and see where it goes from there.

Let's say somebody developed a terraforming kit that could bring life to dead planets and make them livable. They need a chief architect – that's you – in charge of overseeing the details ... everything about the colony, right down to the economic system. And they're building it from scratch.

In order to complete this, you'll have to give some thought to what pieces fit together to make a "good society". What ideas, principles, and values will help you navigate any hard decisions that are going to come up in such a project. You'll need them for some way to measure your success, too.

As we go through this, we'll look at seven questions. How you answer them will shape the framework of your new Society 2.0.

You'll notice as we unpack these questions that we'll look at ideas that might seem so basic that we all know what they mean. But you will find these words – like freedom or fairness – will mean very different things to different people.

You will find that these questions are exactly the sort of thing that Fans and Doubters would disagree on, which makes them a very good place to start.

Chapter 2 - Freedom

What'll be the first thing to happen when you get the Chief Architect job for this Deep Space colony? You'll get advice, of course! Every stranger will be an instant expert on all the things you will need to do. Every other sentence will start with an "If I were you–".

People will tell you all the awesome things you need to include in the designs, and somewhere near the top of that list will be the word "freedom".

That's a no-brainer right? Of course freedom is important! Ok, hotshot, try to define freedom in a way that makes everybody happy. It's harder than you think. Just because everybody thinks they know what freedom means, doesn't mean they all mean the same thing.

The anarchist thinks freedom should let him do whatever, whenever to whomever. How's that gonna fly in your little world? Didn't think so. You'd be *Lord of the Flies* before you knew it. Turns out that restrictions to our freedoms can be a good thing. But that isn't the only hiccup.

If you look at freedom from different times and places, they mean very different things. The check MLK Jr. marched to Washington for is a different freedom than the "Peace, land, bread" Lenin promised the Russian peasants. The freedom the Mayflower pilgrims were looking for was different from France's "Liberty! Equality! Fraternity!"

Whose definition are we playing with here?

It depends if you're playing with the Fans or the Doubters. This is their first point of conflict, they view freedom (or rights) differently. The Fans prefer Protective freedoms, and the Doubters prefer Permissive freedoms. (Our use of freedom will be informal, not the philosophically rigorous definitions.)

What makes them different?

We'll start with the Doubters. They want the right to be left alone. Police can't walk into your house uninvited. People can't tell you to shut up when they disagree with you. You can't be confined without cause. People can't tell you what to think, what philosophy or religion to embrace, or what friends to choose. These are the freedoms you have whether you're rich or poor, wise or foolish. The only way you can lack them is if someone takes them from you by force.

The Fans' freedoms work differently. It's a list of things that everyone can expect to have... with a catch. They only have them after they get them from somewhere. Things that might make the list are food, shelter, medical treatment and a minimum wage. If someone has the ability to get these things for himself, great. But if not, someone else will need to provide it. Lenin's "Peace, Land, Bread" is the kind of language we see with Fans' freedom.

As you can imagine, when times are

hard, people pay more attention to campaigns with these sorts of freedoms in them, then when they think all is well, and they can look after themselves and their families.

Protective freedoms offer people things they are already short on, that are often popular, and can get people elected. Food, homes, jobs (or welfare), and even free phones can be offered to the public. Since generosity and compassion, especially to the needy, are virtues on our culture there is a strong emotional case for such rights.

It's a strong emotional case built on pity. You've heard the pitch, "how can we, who have so much, object to doing our part for the less fortunate?" And the Fans are convinced: a moral government must offer Protective Rights.

So the government gets involved. Bureaucrats identify groups who would need special assistance. Laws and more laws are written. Agencies are set up, and new branches of government are born.

And this is where the Doubters would remind us that the "appeal to pity" is a logical fallacy. Or, to say it differently, "just because it makes you feel good, doesn't make it true." Of course the Doubter would be called heartless or worse before he started pointing out the specific flaws in the Optimist's plan.

He might ask: why not give free everything to everyone? Cars, vacations – you name it! If giving a little is good, isn't giving more better? Or at least food, shelter, utilities, clothes and medicine? Except for a few crazies, even the Fans have a problem with this one. Especially if they can do math.

Doubters, then, aren't mean-spirited. They're doing the same thing as the Fans, just with different numbers. Which means they can have a sensible discussion about how much is too much without being called Scrooge. The real question is where to draw the line, and they'd ask it this way:

Since it's hopeless to meet everybody's needs with limited resources and almost unlimited need, is it better to meet everyone's needs badly, or a few people's needs well? Why not use the triage system for prioritizing needs. The real needy will get the help first, and everyone else can look into the other options, taking direct or indirect responsibility for their own needs – if they are really needs. What's wrong with providing for themselves, when possible, or leaning on others (family, friends, charities) when they can't.

And notice how charities don't dry up when the government isn't funding them? Not all of them anyway. That's the second point.

Whenever someone says "it's the government's job to provide (fill in the blank)", there is a question you can ask. What happens if they can't provide it? Sometimes governments go bankrupt, or just don't have the budget. What happens to the needy then? Well, that depends...

Again, it will work like hospital triage. Trivial things will be ignored. People will mobilize around the causes they find important, and form groups to make them happen – service groups for example, already do this. Some situations will be handled by family and friends. Families can get really creative with solutions when they need to; love and friendship are powerful motivators with these sort of things.

Needs that can't be met in these ways will turn to the kindness of strangers (things like churches and soup kitchens). By this point, the frivolous needs have been separated from the serious ones and the government – if no other options are available – might step in to help the few who are left.

Third point, how would you even make Protective rights work? Looking around, we can already see enormous, inefficient, paperwork-choked social systems that can't keep their own promises to "help people". How do we know new ones will do better? Supposing they don't, should we make another one after that? Can you shut down a government program that fails to do the job, or wastes money on proverbial $500 hammers? Good luck with that.

Here's the real problem: perpetual compulsory support. Suppose a group was a spectacular failure, wasteful and inept. How can it die a natural death? That depends on its funding source.

With a charity that gets money only

from the public, that's easy. If charities go corrupt, for instance, people walk away and take their money with them. This by itself is sometimes enough to keep charities honest – people don't like wastiing their hard-earned money.

That changes when the government's paying the bills. Long after everyone's forgotten why the agency was formed in the first place, it will keep putting its hand in the taxpayer's pocket.

Finally, the Doubters would remind us that "political people make political decisions". This means whoever's in charge will have pet projects and favorite groups that will get special treatment whether or not it's justified. Biases change over time, but will never go away.

For example, service groups that have no religious ties are currently preferred by government – not because the service delivered is measured against their religious counterparts, but because they are irreligious. This ignores the record religious groups tend to have for helping needy, especially at the local level.

Enshrining protective rights will tie

these rights into a political system, which uses what was intended for the good of its citizens as political carrots and sticks leveraged by backroom deals and political hacks. That's inefficient, unfair, and wasteful.

※⁂※

CHAPTER 3 - FAILURE

PROTECTIVE RIGHTS OR NO, LIFE will kick you in the teeth sometimes. Bad Things will happen. And when life in your deep space colony falls apart – as it sometimes will – what will you do with the pieces?

Bad Things come in all shapes and sizes, and might hit you in your body or mind, riches or relationships; or it can hit a whole crowd of people at once with epidemics, crop failures, floods or war. We make fun of ancient religious rituals to appease the "Bad Thing" and keep them from happening, but we spend billions on supplements to do the same thing. Maybe we're the crazy ones.

Even the Fans can tell you that government can't wish away fire, flood or famine. What do we do about problems we can't just "wish away"?

Page one of their playbook would say – "have the government fix it." What would that look like?

They would want to anticipate problems, and provide an escape hatch, parachute, or crash mat for every dangerous situation, preferably before anyone gets hurt. Unemployment needs staff retraining; illiterate kids should pass the grade anyway. The government's trump card for this task is "make new laws".

You've got your laws for food safety, home safety, play safety, and safety-safety. If they notice something not yet registered, mandated or legislated they will start a study to determine what new laws are needed.

Just some advice ... watch yourself around the people who take safety super-seriously. They have no sense of humor. If you were to joke that kids should wear a rappelling harness on the playground slide, they might implement it. Or maybe ban the slide. They're the guys with sour faces and gruff tones at airport security patting down granny in her wheelchair, and confiscating whichever brand of deodorant wasn't on this week's approved list.

Think I'm kidding? Plug "illegal lemonade stand" as search terms into your browser and see for yourself.

Fans wouldn't mind if the government bandaged every skinned knee, and kissed the boo-boo better ... and better still, if they could prevent the fall in the first place.

Fans might never think of "failure" as an engine of progress. a painful but powerful teacher and a crucible of the human spirit. Their determination to put training wheels on life to protect us from its hardships tells us something. They don't think the human spirit is rough-and-ready. It is perhaps fragile and brittle, like fine china. Maybe that's why they treat reality as a harsh and bitter thing-we-need-protection-from.

Of course, that's how their critics would say it. Fans would object and say they are being perfectly reasonable. Who doesn't want to keep kids safe from broken bones and bullies. Why should only the wealthy and well-connected get a do-over when business deals go south? Why should the best job prospects be closed to you just because you sank your time and money into a degree in gender studies?

It's a Wonderful Life did a thought experiment of it's own. It, too, played with the "what if" question. Clarence shows George how life would be different had he never been born.

What if we tried that same idea on the Risk and Pain and Bad Things that happen in the world? Let's look at a few significant moments in history where Risk and Pain and Bad Things were happening, and put you in a position to make choices at the fork in the road.

Let's throw out a few real-world examples, and see where it takes us.

Here's one: a young man – in his teens – was diagnosed with cancer and lost his leg. He organized an event to raise awareness for his condition, but died before he could complete it. He was only 22. Was it wasted life? Maybe … except that his name was Terry Fox, and his attempt to run the width of Canada on an artificial leg started an annual run that has raised more than $500 million for medical research internationally, and has inspired innumerable copycats. Should we wish away his troubles? It would also mean wishing away the medical research those runs made possible.

Here's another: countless people throw away their lives testing some guy's crackpot invention. Would improved safety rules prevent their deaths? Sure it would. Do you enforce strict safety rules?

If you said yes, you have saved many test pilots from death and dismemberment. But the price you will pay is the loss of modern aviation, space exploration, satellites, communication and any scientific or medical breakthrough that ever relied on low-gravity experimentation. Everyone, and all trade will now rely on surface travel. And just like that, our modern economy is knocked back about a century.

What about education? Students quit, or flunk out all the time. Should we make it impossible to flunk out? Would you make the dropouts stay in school? Then they wouldn't launch computer empires out of their homes. What about bullying? Do you want to make sure that nobody is mistreated for having a minority opinion? Then nobody would have fled persecution on the Mayflower.

Here's a political hot-button issue: should businessmen be allowed to make big profits if it means cutting back workers?

One Mr. Hargreaves made innovations in his company and workers were afraid of being laid off. His own employees broke into his house to destroy his labor-saving inventions. Hargreaves rebuilt them and had them broken again ... this time by the competitors he was out-performing. Should you side with the businessman, the workers, or the competitors? Was there an unfair advantage, and should it be stopped? If you sided against Hargreaves, say goodbye to the Spinning Jennies ... and the Industrial Revolution ... and modern automation.

Edison obviously knew a thing or two about failure. You already know his "how not to make a lightbulb" quote. But maybe this one will be new to you:

"Restlessness is discontent and discontent is the first necessity of progress. Show me a thoroughly satisfied man and I will show you a failure."

A successful inventor who had "failed" so many times didn't see failure the way others do. To him, failure wasn't defined as falling short of a goal; it was not trying in the first place. Hockey legend Wayne Gretzky said it this way, "You miss 100% of the shots you do not take."

The worst case scenario – if you ask the Fans – is in trying to do something and having it not work out. Their ideal government would protect us from such risks.

But to the Doubters, that sort of failure is "just a setback". It's far worse in a sterile world where you are the cog in someone else's machine. Worse would be a situation in which nothing you do really matters.

Worse, for the Doubter, is the government-mandated velvet rope that forbids wanderers from charting their own course. Worse, for the Doubter, is being forced to stay on a beaten path with no real shot at spectacular success – because the greatest high-rolling success stories happen more when there's something to lose.

Chapter 4 - Future

ANY SELF-RESPECTING SCI-FI ILlustration will have something to say about time. No, we're not talking about quantum physics, wormholes or paradoxes, don't worry. But we will need to plan for the future.

Here's your scenario. Earth Prime is a long way off, much too far for trade or supplies. You're pretty much on your own out here. Your freshly-minted little world has everything you need, but it'll be some time before everything is up and running the way it should be. Right now it's still a pioneer's paradise: untamed and wild. Progress will start slowly, because you still have to set up food, roads, resources, manufacturing and all the rest. Your world also has several small moons on it, one of which just happens to be rich in that unique resource, "Mineral Z".

"Mineral Z" is a very rare and valuable resource, without which Interstellar travel will be completely impossible.

Here's your dilemma. There's another human colony in a nearby Solar System. This one is just close enough to trade with. It was started before yours, and has already modernized. They give you an offer ... but should you take it?

Here's the offer. They will help you modernize your colony in months rather than generations. They will help you fast-track into a modern civilization. They are asking no payment in return. All they want are exclusive mining rights to your undeveloped moon, which, without their help, you won't be advanced enough to mine for at least a generation. They're not unreasonable, they say, and they will give you "a small percentage" of their find as a "good faith" gesture.

This will be another point of conflict between the Fans and the Doubters, one that might not be obvious at first. But it will show up in their different attitudes to "advancement."

If you take the deal, you'll fast-forward into modern society. Teams of experts, engineers and whatever will organize and execute the transformation. You'll be up-to-the minute in no time. And what a bonus! It won't cost you anything. At least, nothing tangible.

The only things you are giving up are things you have never truly owned. Since nothing is being taken from your hand, it doesn't actually feel like it cost you anything. There's no wrestling with hard choices, no long-term saving, no delayed gratification. Your homeworld hits the Big-time, and all you give up is something shadowy in the distant future.

And, no surprise, the other side would call this deal insane.

Any gains this shortcut would give them would never measure up to the cost of relinquishing their single most precious resource. The Doubters would be furious if the deal was taken.

The quick route to modern civilization would naturally appeal to the Fans. After all, if you don't have all the extra food production, and buildings and infrastructure that you have back on Earth Prime, how could you provide all the necessities for anyone who needs help? A pioneer world will be stretched pretty thin for resources, and there wouldn't be much overflowing abundance to offer to those with less.

The Doubters, on the other hand, are more likely to embrace the "rugged individualist" model. If he needs something, he'll usually look to ingenuity, his personal network of peers, or free enterprise for the solution. Any job or product he can't provide for himself, he'll barter or buy from someone else. Pulling stumps and bringing order to the untamed wild is something his tribe has been doing for time out of mind.

If you want to know where they really stand on this issue, you might want to imagine the conversation each side would have with their children when your decision was made.

What would the Fans be saying to their kids, if you took the deal? It might be something like this:

"Son, look around. When we got here there was nothing but trees and fields. Now it's a thriving city. We gave you that when we struck The Deal. The Others sent workers here and helped take us from cabins with dirt floors to the towering buildings you see today. The Others even give us some of their Mineral Z, so long as we keep them happy. All this (With a grand sweep of the arms) we did for you, son."

The Doubters wouldn't be quite as happy about the situation. Their speech might look like this:

"Look around son, see those towering buildings? They are the Thirty Pieces of Silver we squandered your future for. They are a daily reminder that our generation wanted the quick fix, and were willing to sell your birthright to get it, because we couldn't see the Big Picture. A few of us stood our ground, but most sold you out for a few comforts of home.

Now some distant planet owns the wealth of that little moon. All the possibilities of wealth and trade and travel locked deep in that moon now belong to strangers, because we didn't want to tame our own wilderness, develop our own cities, and mine our own moon. It's a high price. We get as much Mineral Z as they choose to let us have, and we can't wander the starry skies without it.

Watch how careful our politicians are to never offend them, lest they cut us off. We've enslaved ourselves, and most of us don't even notice. Never forget it, son, and never, *ever* repeat our mistakes."

But if the deal was rejected, the speeches would be almost opposite.

The Fans might launch into the typical "one that got away" speech; the "I coulda been a contendah" lament about the glittering city that never was.

The Doubters, on the other hand, would sound a little like *Braveheart*.

"Son, look around you. Everything you see, we built ourselves. We stand here as free men, owing nothing to anyone. We took no shortcuts, and refused to squander your future for an easier today. If you work hard, your generation will someday go to that moon and take your birthright. We weren't able to finish it all, but we've taken you this far, and now it's your turn. Treasure that birthright, use it wisely, and your descendants will want for nothing. Do not trade it away like we nearly did. One day you will have this talk with your own kids. Will it be like this one, or will it be an apology? Choose wisely."

See how both sides had opposite reactions to the same circumstances? For the Fans an uncertain and distant opportunity was a fair price to pay for immediate gains and gratification. For the Doubters those same immediate gains and gratification were unthinkable. The price was too steep to exchange for the eventual benefit their children would have, even if they never lived to see the day themselves.

We've seen two examples of planning for the future. They are like major purchases. One group will put it on the credit card, and make payments later; the other will "pay-as-you-go". Which model will your world embrace?

Now we've thought about the future. Next up: the harsh reality of the present.

❦

Chapter 5 - Fellow Man

Life is tough. Sometimes things go wrong ... very wrong. People get old, get hurt, or can't "get it together". Sometimes they get blindsided by tragedy. One of the few things in life you can count on is that someone will always need help. And you'll have to plan for that, too. Will the government come riding to the rescue, or will something else kick in?

There are many arguments for building a bigger government, but this is one that really resonates with a lot of people. How many projects were first launched "for the children" or "for the needy"? Think of any program that specifically has the poor, the ill, or anyone called "disadvantaged" as its target. What is said about these programs will often make or break a politician's political future.

The Fans know what's coming next, don't they? They're anticipating the number-crunching about agency staffing and compensation, and maybe some digs about how big a difference these dollars actually make. They might even expect the question whether it might be cheaper to give cash directly to the needy, rather than building another system to waste government dollars. It's all cost-benefit calculation, right?

And they'd have their rebuttal ready. (You may have heard this song before, it goes something like this.)

"Really, Scrooge? What IS one life worth? How many dollars, exactly? Should people starve to save government a buck? Are there no prisons? Are there no workhouses? Let them decrease the surplus population. What, so you can save a buck's worth of taxes, right? That's all you REALLY care about, admit it."

And how much does that tired little dance accomplish, besides both sides getting smug and sanctimonious? Not much. So we'll try another angle.

First, remember that neither side wants to abolish government. Anarchy isn't an option. So we're not discussing "help" or "no help" in black-and-white opposites. We're discussing degrees of help. Who gets how much and when?

Let's look at some principles, before we apply them.

The charity done by your neighbor, service group or religious order is not the same thing as similar work done by the government. There are real differences we should clear up before going any further.

Scenario One

First, how does charity work between friends or family?

They do all sorts of charitable things for each other. Maybe it's a gift of money or necessities. Maybe watching the kids for an evening, fixing a faucet, or showing up on moving day. In one sense, any kindness between people is charity. After all, the word used to mean "love".

Did you notice that kindness was a

gift? There's no guilt, manipulation or self-interest needed when it is freely given out of concern or love for the recipient. Friendships are even enriched by this kind of generosity, because self-sacrifice is involved.

Scenario Two

It changes a little with the stranger on the corner. It's a different dynamic. It becomes more of a sales pitch. Is the story compelling? Do I think he's going to use it to feed an addiction? Am I being manipulated, lied to or pressured? Is there an audience? The motives will be different if the person chooses to give in this situation, and it won't be quite the same warm spontaneous giving you might see between friends.

Scenario Three

The farther removed giver and receiver are, the less personal this exchange becomes. The dynamic changes again when someone asks the government for help. Words like "entitlement" slip into the conversation, and notions like "getting what's mine".

The transaction itself is different. It isn't the voluntary gift of a concerned friend or neighbor anymore. Now it's money collected by government, overseen by a government agent with forms to fill and checklists to follow. It isn't based on generosity; it is simply another government transaction.

This scenario is necessary sometimes. But since it is the least human of the interactions, Doubters would insist it should be the last resort.

In Scenario One, the Giver gave freely without compulsion. It was an expression of kindness, generosity, or concern for someone else. Whatever his reason, the receiver was treated with a humanizing dignity.

In Scenario Two, it was more like a sales transaction. Is the pitch believeable? Is guilt or duty tweaked to pressure me? On the other side, just like any other sales pitch, he makes dozens or hundreds of appeals for "a little money". He will have little, if any, attachment to the givers. They're one among many.

In Scenario Three, the personal relationship is gone. The personal concern for a neighbor is replaced with an agency handling a CATEGORY of people, rather than specific individuals. In fact, it applies mass-production principles and big business models to meeting the needs of the unfortunate.

The "giver" is an employee doing his job. The money he gives is not his own, the government collected (confiscated?) it from others. Taxpayers had no knowledge of what their income would be spent on. So the person giving the money doesn't even get to feel good about helping the needy, because he doesn't know what that money was spent on?

Even the recipient loses in this scenario. He will not see the child or retiree giving up something they can't really spare. So he won't appreciate that what he was given corresponds to someone else doing without.

Instead, he will see a faceless branch of government which – in his mind – might exist only to give handouts. If he gets less, he may feel cheated, though it wasn't his to begin with. If he gets extra, he may not feel grateful, because there is no connection to a real person on the "giving" side of the equation. The transaction has been thoroughly stripped of any "Redemptive" qualities that made the first and second scenarios meaningful.

Fans might suggest that the real world could never have more of the first scenario than the third.

But it can happen, and sometimes does.

If society were arranged in a way that rewarded the families that look after each other (even into old age) and allowing groups (like service and religious groups) to work with minimal interference with taxes and political obstructionism, you might be surprised to see that many people even find joy and fulfillment in giving directly.

And that is how the Doubter would want it.

❦

CHAPTER 6 - FAIRNESS

BUILDING YOUR COLONY IS ONE thing, but if you want to hold it together, you'll need to establish standards on how your colonists can expect to be treated fairly.

"Treat each other fairly"; that's Kindergarten language. How hard could that be? Well, what kind of "fair" do you mean? There are different ways to sort out "fairness".

Do you mean everyone gets equal treatment, no matter what their circumstance or story might be? Rich and Poor, male and female, this or that ethnic group? Or do you mean a different kind of fairness? One that might "tweak the laws" so that those who lag behind get a chance to catch up, or even a head start? Because those models run with very different sets of laws. True, there will probably be times when you have to blend the two systems; but generally, which model will you rely on most?

It might help you picture the difference if you thought in terms of a foot-race. Would you try to make people basically equal at the finish line? Or do they all run the race by the same rules with some finishing far ahead of others? Which sort of equality are you chasing?

Suppose you want to make people equal at the finish line, how do you make it work?

Anyone falling behind will need a chance to catch up. The fastest runners might be called back, or be given a time penalty to even things out. Maybe they'd carry a weighted backpack. Maybe they'd start a little later than the slower runners. Whatever the approach, special rules would be designed to give advantages to certain groups based on what the judges anticipate their disadvantages to be. This will require ongoing assessment and frequent adjustment.

The other option is to let everyone run

under the same conditions. Rules will be stable and predictable, applying equally to all runners. Judges will select no favorites, and whoever is fastest will win, with no apologies to slower runners.

Because these ideas work on opposite principles, you can't really call both models fair. If you think it's fair to give someone a head start, you have already chosen not to put everyone under the same rules. It's an either/or decision. Not surprisingly, when people see the "other" system, they will call it unfair.

How does this play out in the real world?

The answer will be different in different contexts.

In the Legal world, for example, it might show up in sentencing decisions. The question of what the penalty should be will draw from one attitude or the other. If you gave the slower runners a head start, you would also take things like neighborhood, home life, social strata and education into consideration when deciding how the defendant is penalized. If the defendant is from a "high risk" group, your decision may be influenced by those stats. If he's from a poor neighbourhood, lacks education, or has some other disadvantage, you might entertain a lighter sentence.

Alternatively, you would invoke the "justice is blind" approach, and try to decide solely on the facts of the case. You'd not make adjustments (for or against) the defendant based on his identity. Race, religion, education and social status, etc., therefore, must be treated as irrelevant.

The first way has shifting legal goalposts. It offers lenience to one group but not another. The laws of the land would be unequally enforced and based on which group you belong to.

Those who want stable rules call favoritism unkind to the people it is supposed to help. "The soft discrimination of lowered expectations" they might say, is demeaning. Are these people less capable of living up to society's moral standards? Are they somehow morally inferior? If not, why measure them by a lower standard?

Education and the workplace faces the same decision. Do you offer hiring quotas or affirmative action? Some say this makes room to include "unrepresented" people, making a chance for those who might otherwise be denied it.

But the equal rules people would find fault with that, too.

Do they object because some people have to work harder than others to get the same result? Partly, but they would also say it cheapens any real accomplishments of affirmative action recipients. They could never say with confidence, "I did that". They'd face the same doubts and criticisms that a CEO's kid would face as he climbed the corporate ladder in daddy's company.

And what is the message to everyone else? Not everyone can benefit from the affirmative action in school or work. What if you don't get the fast-tracked career path – are you doomed to being mediocre? If you aren't singled out for special treatment by "special people" are you doomed to mediocrity and failure?

We've all seen enough rags-to-riches stories by now to reject that lie, right? Part of what makes life interesting is discovering what you are (and aren't!) good at, and changing your plan accordingly. Not everyone can swim like Phelps, jump like Jordan, write like Twain, invent like Tesla, or think laterally like Einstein. The only way you or I could finish a swim race at the same time as Phelps is if we had a crazy head start. And really, what's the point?

If you wanted to enter a golf cart in a Nascar race, it would be embarrassing. But if you wanted the golf cart to have a shot at winning, the only way to do it is by limiting the real cars so they can only go the golf cart's top speed. The only way to make it fair (in that sense), is to curb excellence. And who really wants to watch a race like that? People come to see the best and the fastest. They don't come to see the first among the mediocre.

Just how far do you take affirmative action? Would you make elite sports teams put one clumsy guy in the big game? Let the guy with a hand tremor be a brain surgeon, because he really, really wants to?

And what about racial preference? That's a sacred cow isn't it? But wait a minute. How are we not at the point where race means nothing, yet? "Race" is an impossibly arbitrary idea. The same media speaks of a man whose mom is Irish and father is African as "the first Black President", called a man with white mother and hispanic father "white".

Are we ready to admit that racial labels suck? We've replaced our black-and white TV's from the 1950's with High Definition. With so much intermingling of cultures from around the world, isn't it time we also replace our 1950's Black-and-White world with today's full spectrum of skin tones?

The interventionist system takes a lot of fine tuning and re-calibrating. What happens if the group you favored at first takes the lead? Do you stop favoring them? Do you flip it again to let another group catch up? To be consistent in your "fairness" you would have to, but chances are, the new inequities will be called payback for past inequalities.

There is yet another complication with using defined groups based on things like skin color or other identifying traits. Doesn't it reject those values for which Dr. Martin Luther King Jr. was most admired: his dream that people will be judged on their character, rather than their skin color?

If you support affirmative action, are you rejecting his dream as unfair?

CHAPTER 7 - FAMILY

IF YOU DIDN'T ALREADY SEE A sharp distinction between the two camps, this next question would help clear that up. This line of thinking could be titled either "family" or "authority". You will soon see that it is one place where our two groups stand the furthest apart.

In small settings, the tension might not be obvious; and, depending on your colony's size, it could even take some time before the topic came up. But squabbling about who's responsible for big decisions eventually will begin, and it's better to have that solved ahead of time. Otherwise, things can get ugly in a hurry. How ugly? Remember how the Declaration of Independence cited their "repeated injuries and usurpations"? It can get THAT kind of ugly.

If you want to know who's on which team, ask this simple question: "who's supposed to be in charge here?" When it's time for the important decision to be made, who will make it? Will it be handled by someone who lives in the neighborhood? Will it be handled by a politician or official halfway around the world?

When the issue of control comes up, we see a tug-of-war. Politicians will often use authority to make people do the "right thing". Governing can be simpler that way. Although not everyone appreciates being told to do the "right thing". Sometimes they object because they think it's none of the government's business in the first place; and sometimes because there's no agreement about what the 'right thing' actually is. When the government can harass, punish, fine, or arrest you for not playing along, it only aggravates the problem.

If you want to see real-world examples of both models, compare the American and Canadian systems. For all their cultural similarities, they have taken opposite rationales to their distribution of power.

In the American Tenth Amendment, the Federal Government has some clearly defined boundaries. Power not explicitly given to the Federal Government belongs to the State. Period. End of story.

The Canadian System reverses that. "Residuary Power" (as it's called) for anything not assigned to the Provinces belongs to the Federal Government.

Are you surprised? Think about it. The American Constitutional Republic draws political authority from "We the People". Since the State is closer to the grassroots level than the Fed, it is given broader powers. The Canadian system is a Constitutional Monarchy. It doesn't draw political authority from "We the People", power flows (in principle) from the Crown. Since the Federal government is more centralized, and nearer the "ruling elites", political power in Canada defaults there.

That conflict is relatively tame, compared to another dimension of this same issue. This one comes much closer to home than rival civic power structures. It cuts straight into every home in the country (or, in your case, colony).

What is the foundational unit of human authority in your culture? In chemistry, everything is built on elements. In biology, life's basic unit is the cell. Where would we locate the foundational unit of authority in our culture?

Where will the buck stop on your world? Are you a grass-roots We-the-People colony, or do you prefer a Crown-Down central authority model? Does the Family have final say, or is the State supreme? When we explore the idea of consent, this last question becomes very important.

Think of a school setting. There will always be some idea too controversial for the classroom. The specific "hot topic" always changes but there will be something, and it's usually linked to a moral/religious/philosophical values conflict between parent and educators.

Which of these describes you? Do you believe the State has a right to ignore or overrule a parent's objections? Then you are putting final authority in the hands of the State. Do you believe parents should have final say on what a child is taught, and should have the right to overrule a government's demands? You have put that authority in the hands of the parent or family.

Maybe you're familiar with the real-world case of Uwe Romeike and his family. They chose to homeschool their kids, and pull them out of the German Public School. Why? Because the classroom was undermining the faith of their children.

According to their Supreme Court, the reason homeschooling is outlawed in Germany is "to counteract the development of religious and philosophically motivated parallel societies". The Romeikes have faced harsh financial penalties and could face having their children taken from them. (If you were wondering, this particular law was established in 1938 under one Adolph Hitler, who obviously used this to his own advantage. As I write this, the law remains in force.)

Who has final say on the instruction of children? We're really asking about indoctrination. Who decides what values or religion the children are raised with or even no religion at all – the Parent, or the State?

Medical consent raises another dilemma. A minor child requires parental consent for almost any medical procedure. Why? Because we believe kids aren't mature enough to weigh the risks and make a rational choice. And yet, certain procedures (fertility-related) are available to young teens without parental consent.

Why should we care?

Legislators are changing laws to overrule parental authority in the life of that minor child. But is it justified? How might either side make their case?

(Pro-state) If a minor is pregnant, or needs testing, a parent might not approve of a medical procedure, and the child will denied access to it. We're just removing unnecessary barriers to the teen getting necessary medical treatment.

(Pro-family) If the State lowers the age of consent for some – but not all – medical procedures, that decision has been driven by politics instead of research and patient well-being. If the child isn't old enough to smoke, drink, use a tanning bed or have a tattoo, what makes them competent to understand medical fine print? Who's to say they understand the risks they are taking on, and aren't getting sketchy advice from unscrupulous practitioners? (Remember Kermit Gosnell?)

What is parental consent supposed to do? Simply, it protects children. In most cases, a parent will love the child and make decisions in his or her best interest. The state has no family bond with the child, might give generic or impersonal advice, and will not have to spend sleepless nights dealing with the consequences of any negative outcomes.

If a government officer makes "the wrong call" he might not even be aware of it. It costs him very little. But a loved one can be affected the rest of their life. Which do you think will usually give the greatest thought to the child's decision?

The group that leans toward the grassroots model is concerned about this impersonal distance between government agents and the patients. They might say it this way:

The difference in how you relate to fellow-citizens or neighbors or family is based on one thing – relationship. Even though you share a country, most citizens are strangers. You have a closer relationship with neighbors – maybe you know them a little, or even well. But family is different. Many people would take a bullet for their family. The big difference in these situations is what kind of a relationship you have to the other person.

So, who should get final say about the care of a minor child? An impersonal stranger who will be unaffected by any tragic choice your kid might make? Or the parent, who will be completely familiar with the medical history of that child, will be responsible for his or her ongoing health, and will share in the consequences – good or ill – that child's decision will create.

It comes down to the question: "Does the government belong to you, or do you belong to government?"

❧❧❦

CHAPTER 8 - FAITH

Have you noticed anything missing in what we've covered so far? We've gone over mechanics and principles of the government you're setting up, but we haven't nailed down what values they'll rely on. We'll need at least *some* idea of right and wrong, won't we?

How are you going to set up the moral structure that your other laws will be a reflection of? Are you going to be hands-off, and let those who govern it decide morality for themselves? That doesn't always work out so well.

Remember the homeschooling family we mentioned earlier? The law that was responsible for their hardship was enacted by the German Third Reich back in 1938. That should be a vivid reminder that people and cultures (even "civilized" ones) are capable of repeating the most horrific mistakes and choices eventually. Eugenics, forced sterilization, internment camps, racism, slave trade, corruption, graft, state-sponsored gangs of thugs intimidating rivals, these were all championed by governments. The potential list of amoral government decisions could be practically endless.

There is another way.

What if you had an apolitical counterweight to the corrupting influence of power? If it were able to challenge the players on the political stage without being one of them, that could be a restraining influence on the misuse of political power? To be effective in that role, they could not have embraced the political pragmatism that so often leads government into choices that suck.

This is exactly the niche that religion (in the broad sense) could fit in. True, not all religions would fit equally well. You would want a religious (or irreligious) philosophy able to give transcendent reasons for the value of human life, fair treatment of each other, respect for people and property, and something consistent with civic order, free speech and a broad spectrum of moral values we already hold dear.

This means the group will need an unwavering reference point for determining good and evil. Stable absolutes will be needed to keep it from drifting into the same errors that public opinion and the state and public will need corrected. It would also help if this group has a mechanism for identifying and rejecting corrupt leaders in its own ranks.

We have something like that already. Well, we used to. Right now it sucks just like everything else we've talked about. But much of "Western Culture" as we know it, including many of the values on the list were gifts from a Christianized culture.

It might be hard to believe for some of you that a lot of the cultural, social, moral and legal framework that makes us "enlightened" came straight out of the Christian worldview.

That doesn't mean that Christianity is the only counterweight to government missteps. You could always look for other transcendent reference points, but any replacement would need to do an equal or better job than historical Christianity did by providing a framework for the liberties we enjoy today.

Here are some others that have been tried elsewhere.

In places like China, you can be imprisoned for speaking out against the government. Their government's moral choices, even on issues like infanticide, arresting of dissidents and forced sterilizations are not up for discussion. There is no room for dissenting opinions in a system like that.

Islam is different again. Religious leaders are calling the shots, which means they are politically involved. How does anyone give impartial arms-length criticism of their own failings? They don't.

Today's Christianity is dismissed as vapid and lightweight. And it should be. It's a long way from the robust faith that once shaped Western Culture. Now they're so busy being "inoffensive and liked" that they've stopped being "salt and light". But it hasn't always been like this.

There was a time when people like Wilberforce, Bonhoffer, John Wesley and William Booth dramatically reformed their cultures. Did you realize that John Knox's universal education in Scotland was the predecessor to today's public education?

From their earliest history, Christians have stood apart from government leaders and called them out when they got things wrong. Sometimes it cost them their lives. Also from earliest times, they showed kindness to those nobody else cared about: they took in abandoned children, cared for plague victims (and often died of it themselves), fed widows and welcomed slaves as equals.

The choice for our moral framework either requires us to trust leadership to police themselves from any excesses or abuses, or (if you believe Acton's "Power Corrupts" adage) you will want someone to step up and play the role the Church played (sometimes better than others) for centuries.

❧❦❧

CONCLUSION

NOW WE'VE FINISHED OUR thought experiment, and can apply what we've learned to real-world situations.

As you will remember, we have discussed Freedom, and the contrasting definitions; Failure, and how to respond to it; Future, and whether deferred payment makes for good policy; Fellow Man, and the needs of the less fortunate; Fairness, comparing equalized results with uniform treatment under law; Family (or authority), and whether authority should flow from the top down, or the bottom up; and Faith - what corrective mechanism, if any, should critique the moral failings of our leaders, or even culture itself.

As we go down these lists, two very different "ideal" cultures take shape.

The first is a hands-on government. The government will be responsible for keeping peace and order with explicit regulations or remedies for nearly every situation. People earning too little will be subsidized by those who are not. Success and failure will be moderated by third parties. Consents-for-this-or-that will be granted by governments, rather than parents, and faith can be privately held, but seldom seen in public.

The second model lets government stand aside whenever it isn't really needed. It prefers stopping a bad law to passing a good one. Small groups and families will be free to live by their own conscience and value systems, unless they violate someone else's person or property. The government will protect the public from lawbreakers, but will also encourage the public to give proactive help in times of hardship – either directly, or through charity. Laws would be written with the intention of stability and clarity, in language understood by ordinary citizens, with no obligations for different groups to play by different rules.

Maybe this process led you to different categories and conclusions. Maybe your ideas challenged or even contradicted the ones presented. That's okay. The point was not to make you think like the author. The point was to provide new approaches to help grapple with these ideas for ourselves, chopping them down to a manageable size, rather than passively absorbing what someone else tells you to believe.

As we conclude this exercise, let's revisit the original names we gave the groups, and try to tag them with something more accurate.

The Fans support direct government involvement in daily life. Larger, centralized systems are preferred to smaller, independent ones; they would be more likely to support, for example, the UN. Massive debt deferring payment to future generations is justifiable. Arcane systems of laws giving some citizens advantages that are unavailable to other citizens is called a solution to inequalities.

The expense of such a large government is unavoidable and necessary, so it is reasonable to expect the "well-off" to shoulder some additional cost. In each of these, the common denominator is the prominent role of government in daily life.

A more precise term for the Fans might be "Interventionists".

Where the Interventionists zigged, the "Doubters" zagged. They try to keep government from meddling in any area of life that isn't justifiable. They are concerned about programs spending money their kids and grandkids will have to pay back. They want laws that are uniform, and relatively independent of the whims and wishes of whoever enforces them. When possible, private charities are preferred above government assistance programs.

Excessive taxes are thought confiscatory, a curtailment of personal freedom, and a violation of property rights. Government should spend its energy and resources only on certain specific tasks, and get out of the way so the public can handle the rest. Doubters are suspicious of Interventionists, would view them as sellouts; and might call them "Totalitarians" or "Oligarchs" because they concentrate great power in the hands of very few.

How would the Doubters describe themselves? Minimalists might be accurate, or maybe an equivalent term that expresses the conviction that they are free citizens granting consent to the government, not slaves who scrape and bow before it.

While this was just a theoretical model, it gave us a forum to test drive rival ideas of how to manage a society. Such thinking leads us to more comprehensive – and less patchy – solutions for facing problems we see today. It lets us imagine an integrated model of the societies running on each value system, so we can evaluate them ourselves.

This exercise was about persuasion, not coercion. Embrace whichever model you find more appealing. Some of you might share my Minimalist preferences. Others might side with the Interventionists. Either way, I hope this exercise helps us think through relevant ideas to a higher level, and gives us language to express our convictions and differences.

And maybe, once in awhile, our political discourse can trade more ideas than insults.

Wes Walker is a Christian husband and father of three, bringing the Clash Attitude to Canada's Capital. When not writing submissions for Clash, he is involved in Church, his children's school, and is pursuing interests in Theology, History, and Philosophy.

Other Books by White Feather Press

Raising Boys Feminists Will Hate
(by Doug Giles)

Raising Righteous and Rowdy Girls
(by Doug Giles)

Sandy Hook Massacre - When Seconds Count Police are Minutes Away
(by Doug Giles and other
ClashDaily.com authors)

*RKBA: Defending the Right to Keep
and Bear Arms*
(by Skip Coryell)

By Force of Patriots
(by Cameron Reddy)

www.ingramcontent.com/pod-product-compliance
Lightning Source LLC
Chambersburg PA
CBHW050557280326
41933CB00011B/1887